FIRST 50 SONGS

YOU SHOULD PLAY ON THE TUBA

ISBN 978-1-5400-7008-1

Visit Hal Leonard Online at
www.halleonard.com

Contact us:
Hal Leonard
7777 West Bluemound Road
Milwaukee, WI 53213
Email: info@halleonard.com

In Europe, contact:
Hal Leonard Europe Limited
42 Wigmore Street
Marylebone, London, W1U 2RN
Email: info@halleonardeurope.com

In Australia, contact:
Hal Leonard Australia Pty. Ltd.
4 Lentara Court
Cheltenham, Victoria, 3192 Australia
Email: info@halleonard.com.au

ALL OF ME

Tuba

Words and Music by JOHN STEPHENS
and TOBY GAD

Slowly, in 2

ALL YOU NEED IS LOVE

Tuba

Words and Music by JOHN LENNON
and PAUL McCARTNEY

AMAZING GRACE

TUBA

Traditional American Melody

BASIN STREET BLUES

TUBA

Words and Music by
SPENCER WILLIAMS

BEST SONG EVER

Tuba

Words and Music by EDWARD DREWETT,
WAYNE HECTOR, JULIAN BUNETTA
and JOHN RYAN

BEER BARREL POLKA

(Roll Out the Barrel)

Based on the European success "Skoda Lasky"*

Tuba

By LEW BROWN, WLADIMIR A. TIMM,
JAROMIR VEJVODA and VASEK ZEMAN

CARNIVAL OF VENICE

TUBA

By JULIUS BENEDICT

Moderately, with motion

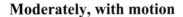

CIRCLE OF LIFE
from THE LION KING

Tuba

Music by ELTON JOHN
Lyrics by TIM RICE

Moderately (with an African beat)

DOWN ON THE CORNER

TUBA

Words and Music by
JOHN FOGERTY

THE ELEPHANT
from CARNIVAL OF THE ANIMALS

TUBA

By CAMILLE SAINT-SAËNS

Allegretto pomposo

(small note optional)

EVERMORE
from BEAUTY AND THE BEAST

Music by ALAN MENKEN
Lyrics by TIM RICE

TUBA

Sturdy Ballad

FLY ME TO THE MOON
(In Other Words)

Tuba

Words and Music by
BART HOWARD

FIGHT SONG

TUBA

Words and Music by RACHEL PLATTEN
and DAVE BASSETT

THE FOOL ON THE HILL

Words and Music by JOHN LENNON
and PAUL McCARTNEY

Tuba

GOD BLESS AMERICA®

Words and Music by
IRVING BERLIN

TUBA

Moderately

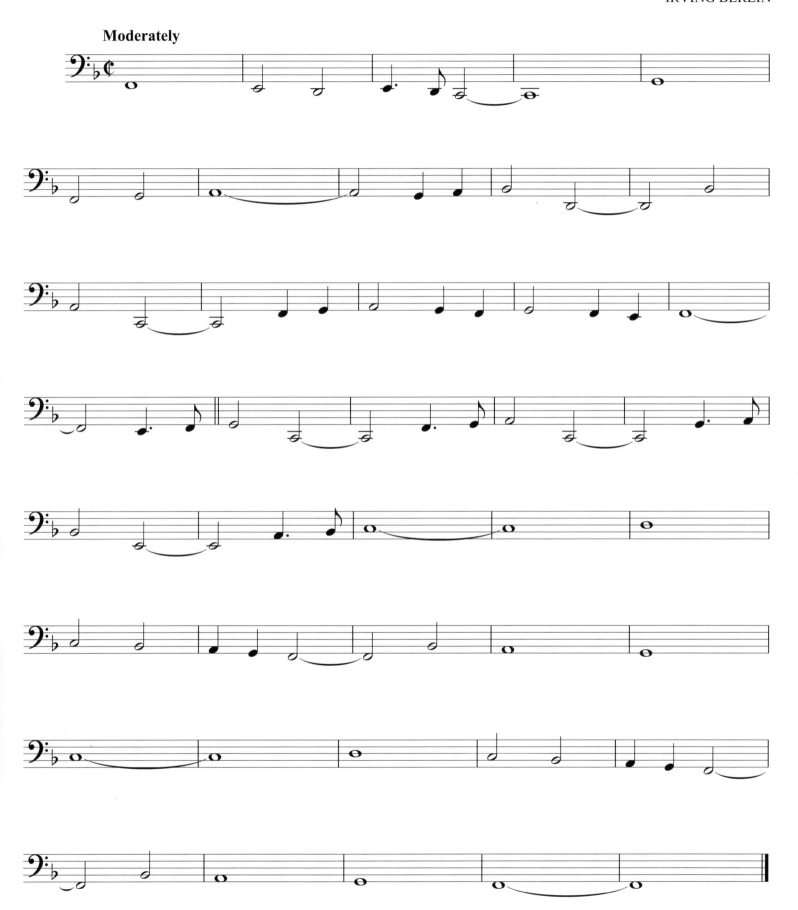

THE GODFATHER
(Love Theme)
from the Paramount Picture THE GODFATHER

Tuba

By NINO ROTA

Slowly and expressively

HALLELUJAH

Words and Music by
LEONARD COHEN

Tuba

Moderately slow, in 2

HAPPY
from DESPICABLE ME 2

Words and Music by
PHARRELL WILLIAMS

TUBA

Moderately fast

HELLO

TUBA

Words and Music by
LIONEL RICHIE

HELLO, DOLLY!

from HELLO, DOLLY!

Tuba

Music and Lyric by
JERRY HERMAN

HEY JUDE

TUBA

Words and Music by JOHN LENNON
and PAUL McCARTNEY

HOW DEEP IS YOUR LOVE
from the Motion Picture SATURDAY NIGHT FEVER

Tuba

Words and Music by BARRY GIBB,
ROBIN GIBB and MAURICE GIBB

Moderately

I WILL ALWAYS LOVE YOU

Tuba

Words and Music by
DOLLY PARTON

IN THE HALL OF THE MOUNTAIN KING

from PEER GYNT

By EDVARD GRIEG

TUBA

THEME FROM "JAWS"

from the Universal Picture JAWS

Tuba

By JOHN WILLIAMS

Moderately

Repeat and Fade

JUST GIVE ME A REASON

Tuba

Words and Music by ALECIA MOORE,
JEFF BHASKER and NATE RUESS

CODA

JUST THE WAY YOU ARE

Tuba

Words and Music by BRUNO MARS,
ARI LEVINE, PHILIP LAWRENCE,
KHARI CAIN and KHALIL WALTON

Moderately

LET IT GO
from FROZEN

TUBA

Music and Lyrics by KRISTEN ANDERSON-LOPEZ
and ROBERT LOPEZ

LIVIN' ON A PRAYER

Tuba

Words and Music by JON BON JOVI,
DESMOND CHILD and RICHIE SAMBORA

Moderate Rock

Repeat and Fade

MAS QUE NADA

Words and Music by
JORGE BEN

TUBA

MY HEART WILL GO ON
(Love Theme from 'Titanic')
from the Paramount and Twentieth Century Fox Motion Picture TITANIC

Tuba

Music by JAMES HORNER
Lyric by WILL JENNINGS

THE PINK PANTHER
from THE PINK PANTHER

By HENRY MANCINI

Tuba

Moderately, mysterioso

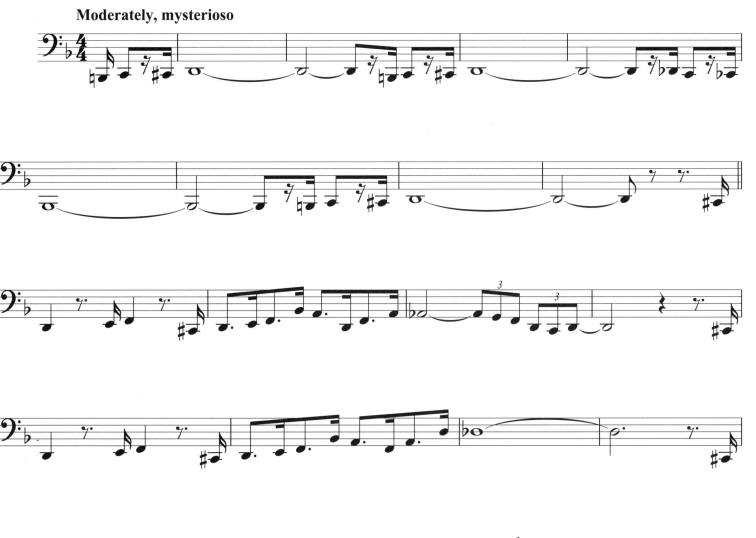

NIGHT TRAIN

Tuba

Words by OSCAR WASHINGTON
and LEWIS C. SIMPKINS
Music by JIMMY FORREST

PETER GUNN
Theme Song from the Television Series

By HENRY MANCINI

TUBA

PURE IMAGINATION
from WILLY WONKA AND THE CHOCOLATE FACTORY

Tuba

Words and Music by LESLIE BRICUSSE
and ANTHONY NEWLEY

ROAR

Tuba

Words and Music by KATY PERRY,
MAX MARTIN, DR. LUKE,
BONNIE McKEE and HENRY WALTER

Moderately

ROLLING IN THE DEEP

Tuba

Words and Music by ADELE ADKINS
and PAUL EPWORTH

SATIN DOLL

Tuba

By DUKE ELLINGTON

SEE YOU AGAIN

from FURIOUS 7

Tuba

Words and Music by CAMERON THOMAZ,
CHARLIE PUTH, JUSTIN FRANKS,
ANDREW CEDAR, DANN HUME,
JOSH HARDY and PHOEBE COCKBURN

SHAKE IT OFF

TUBA

Words and Music by TAYLOR SWIFT,
MAX MARTIN and SHELLBACK

THE SORCERER'S APPRENTICE
(Theme)
from FANTASIA

TUBA

By PAUL DUKAS

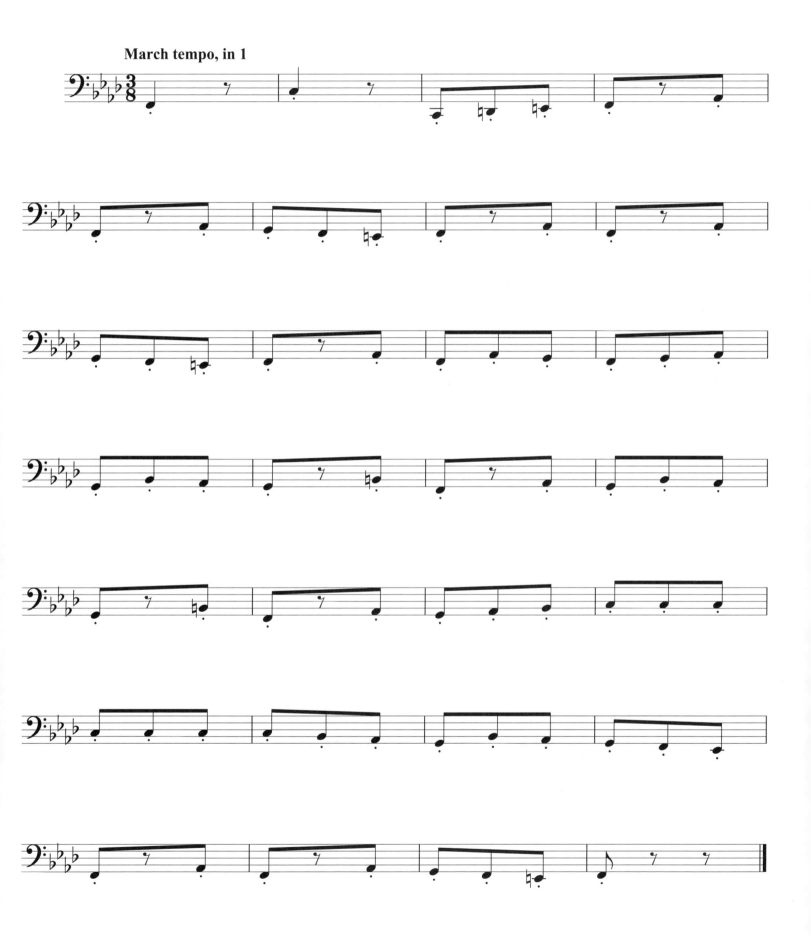

STAND BY ME

Words and Music by JERRY LEIBER,
MIKE STOLLER and BEN E. KING

Tuba

THE STAR-SPANGLED BANNER

Tuba

Words by FRANCIS SCOTT KEY
Music by JOHN STAFFORD SMITH

With spirit

STAY WITH ME

Tuba

Words and Music by SAM SMITH,
JAMES NAPIER, WILLIAM EDWARD PHILLIPS,
TOM PETTY and JEFF LYNNE

STOMPIN' AT THE SAVOY

Tuba

By BENNY GOODMAN,
EDGAR SAMPSON and CHICK WEBB

Bright Swing

STRANGERS IN THE NIGHT

Words by CHARLES SINGLETON and EDDIE SNYDER
Music by BERT KAEMPFERT

Tuba

Moderately slow

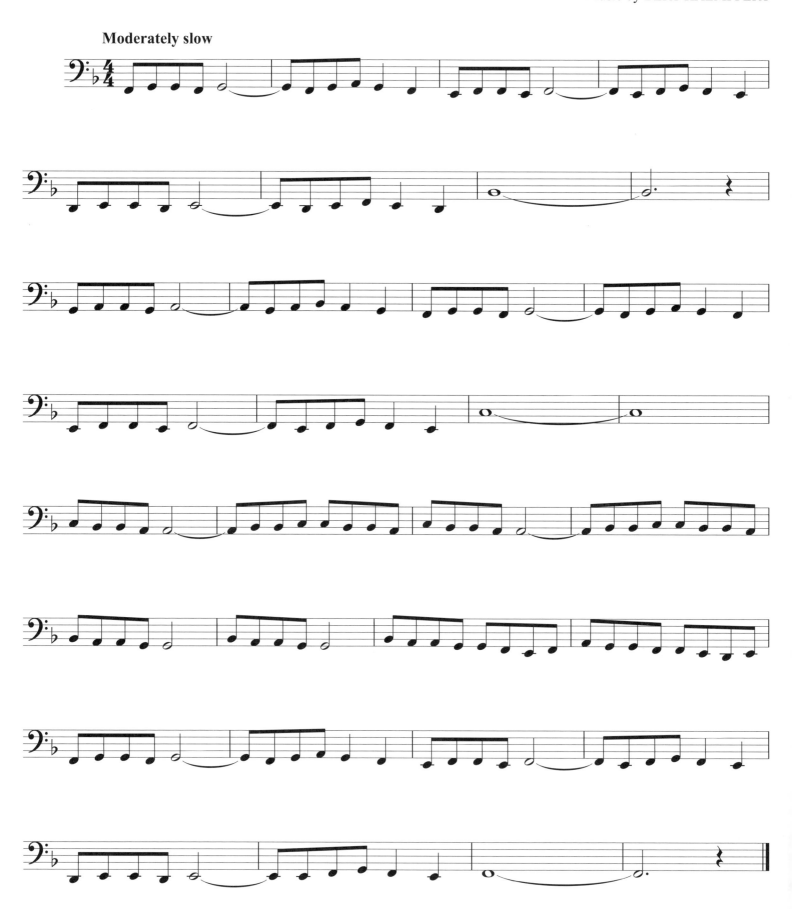

SUMMERTIME

from PORGY AND BESS®

Tuba

Music and Lyrics by GEORGE GERSHWIN,
DuBOSE and DOROTHY HEYWARD
and IRA GERSHWIN

THIS IS ME
from THE GREATEST SHOWMAN

TUBA

Words and Music by BENJ PASEK
and JUSTIN PAUL

Defiantly

UPTOWN FUNK

Tuba

Words and Music by MARK RONSON,
BRUNO MARS, PHILIP LAWRENCE, JEFF BHASKER, DEVON GALLASPY,
NICHOLAUS WILLIAMS, LONNIE SIMMONS, RONNIE WILSON,
CHARLES WILSON, RUDOLPH TAYLOR and ROBERT WILSON

Moderately

WHAT A WONDERFUL WORLD

Tuba

Words and Music by GEORGE DAVID WEISS
and BOB THIELE